How To Swim

Backstroke

a step-by-step guide for beginners
learning backstroke technique

Mark Young

Author Online!

For more resources and swimming help visit
Mark Young's website at

www.swim-teach.com

Mark Young is a well-established swimming instructor with over twenty years experience of teaching thousands of adults and children to swim. He has taken nervous, frightened children and adults with a fear of water and made them happy and confident swimmers.   He has also turned many of average ability into advanced swimmers. This book draws on his experiences and countless successes to put together this simplistic methodical approach to swimming.

Also by Mark Young

Step-By-Step Guides
How To Swim Breaststroke
How To Swim Front Crawl
How To Swim Butterfly

How To Be A Swimming Teacher
The Definitive Guide to Becoming a
Successful Swimming Teacher

A Catalogue record for this book is available from the British Library

ISBN 9780992742850

Published by: Educate & Learn Publishing, Hertfordshire, UK

Graphics by Mark Young, courtesy of Poser V6.0

Design and typeset by Mark Young

Published in association with www.swim-teach.com

Contents

Page

How to use this book

Learning how to swim can be a frustrating experience sometimes, especially for an adult. Kick with your legs, pull with your arms, breathe in, and breathe out and do it all at the right time. Before you know it you've got a hundred and one things to think about and do all at the same time or in the right sequence.

How To Swim Backstroke is designed to break the stroke down into its component parts, those parts being body position, legs, arms, breathing and timing and coordination. An exercise or series of exercises are then assigned to that part along with relevant teaching points and technique tips, to help focus only on that stroke part.

The exercises form a reference section for the stroke, complete with technique tips, teaching points and common mistakes for each individual exercise.

What exactly are these exercises?

Each specific exercise focuses on a certain part of the swimming stroke, for example the body position, the leg kick, the arms, the breathing or the timing and coordination, all separated into easy to learn stages. Each one contains a photograph of the exercise being performed, a graphical diagram and all the technique elements and key focus points that are relevant to that particular exercise.

How will they help?

They break down your swimming technique into its core elements and then force you to focus on that certain area. For example if you are performing a leg kick exercise, the leg kick is isolated and therefore your focus and concentration is only on the legs. The technical information and key focus points then fix your concentration on the most important elements of the leg kick. The result: a more efficient and technically correct leg kick. The same then goes for exercises for the arms, breathing, timing and coordination and so on.

Will they help to learn and improve your swimming strokes?

Yes, definitely! Although it is not the same as having a swimming teacher with you to correct you, these practical exercises perfectly compliment lessons or help to enhance your practice time in the pool. They not only isolate certain areas but also can highlight your bad habits. Once you've worked though each element of the stroke and practiced the exercises a few times, you will slowly eliminate your bad habits. The result: a more efficient and technically correct swimming stroke, swum with less effort!

8

Backstroke

technique overview

This is the most efficient stroke swum on the back and is the third fastest of all swimming strokes. The majority of the power is produced by the alternating arm technique and its horizontal streamlined body position gives it its efficiency. Therefore this is the preferred stroke in competitive races swum on the back.

The nature of floating on the back, face up (supine) can be a calming and relaxing feeling. Also the face is clear of the water, allowing easy breathing and little water splashes onto the face. On the other hand it can be counter productive at first, as it can give a feeling of disorientation and unease, as the person is facing upwards and therefore unaware of their surroundings. The supine body position is flat and horizontal, with ears slightly below the water surface.

The legs kick in an alternating action, continuously up and down to help balance the action of the arms. This stroke has two different arm actions: the bent arm pull, which is the most efficient, and the straight arm pull, which is the easiest to learn. Therefore the straight arm pull is best for beginners.

Breathing should be in time with recovery of each arm, breathing in with one arm recovery and out with the other. Ideally there should be 6 leg kicks to one arm cycle but the stroke timing may vary according to the swimmer's level of coordination.

Body Position

The supine body position for this stroke is flat and horizontal, with ears slightly below the water surface.

Good floaters will find this position relaxing and relatively easy, whereas poor floaters will find it difficult to achieve a comfortable head position.

Body position remains horizontal and relaxed

The head remains still throughout the stroke with the eyes looking slightly down the body at a point the swimmer is swimming away from.

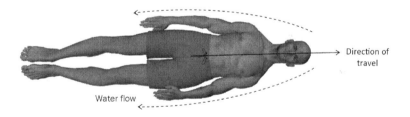

The head position is important because a raised head makes it more difficult to keep the hips raised in the correct position, which leads to a sitting type position in the water.

The hips and shoulders remain at or near the water surface but roll with the stroke. The legs and feet should be extended and remain together to maximise efficiency, with knees remaining below the water surface.

Common body position mistakes

Ever get that feeling that you are sinking when you swim on your back? It is very common to allow the legs to drop and the body position to become angled in the water without knowing it is happening. This is usually caused either by allowing the hips to drop or lifting the head slightly or a combination of both. As the legs drop deeper the whole stroke becomes less efficient and more energy consuming.

Performing a push and glide from holding the poolside is a good way of testing how flat you can remain. Ensure that you look upwards as you push away and stretch out so that your hips, legs and feet rise to the surface. The overall body position is easily maintained with a correct and efficient leg kick.

Leg Kick

During this stroke the legs kick in an alternating action, continuously up and down to help balance the action of the arms.

Legs should be stretched out with toes pointed (plantar flexed) and ankles should be relaxed and loose with toes pointing slightly inwards.

The amount of propulsion generated from the kick will depend on the size of the feet, ankle mobility and strength of the legs.

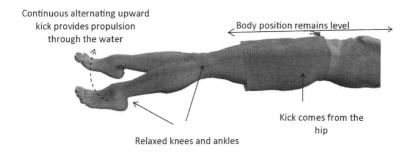

Continuous alternating upward kick provides propulsion through the water

Body position remains level

Kick comes from the hip

Relaxed knees and ankles

The knee should bend slightly and then straighten as the leg kicks upwards. Toes should kick to create a small splash but not break the water surface.

During specific leg practices the legs kick in a vertical plane. However, the arm action causes the body to roll making the legs kick part sideways, part vertical and partly to the other side.

13

Common leg kick mistakes

The most common fault with the leg kick during backstroke is closely related to the body position, when the swimmer allows their legs to sink below the water surface. The toes should just break the water surface and the legs kick from the hip with a slight bend at the knee.

An easy exercise to help maintain leg kick technique at the correct level in the water is to hold a float or kick board across the chest and perform the leg kick. The float will provide support so that the swimmer can focus on kicking up towards the water surface whilst maintaining a level head and level hips. Only then will the leg kick be at its most efficient.

There are two possible arm actions for backstroke. The bent arm pull, which is more effective because it is faster and has greater propulsion, and the straight arm pull used in more recreational backstroke.

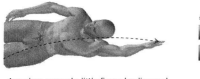

Arm rises upwards, little finger leading and arm brushing the ear

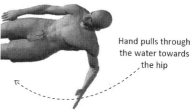

Hand pulls through the water towards the hip

straight arm pull

entry
The arm should be straight and as inline with the shoulder as possible. The hand should be turned with palm facing outwards and little finger entering the water first.

propulsive phase
The arm sweeps through the water in a semi-circle, pulling with force just under the water surface, pulling to the outside of the thigh.

recovery
The thumb or the back of the hand should exit the water first. The shoulders roll again with the shoulder of the recovering arm rolling upwards. The arm rotates through 180 degrees over the shoulder. The palm is turned outwards during recovery to ensure that the hand enters the water little finger first.

bent arm pull

As the arm pulls through to completion, the overall path should follow an 'S' shape.

entry
The entry is the same as the straight arm pull, with the little finger entering first, the palm facing out and the arm close to the shoulder line.

downward sweep
The palm should always face the direction of travel. The shoulders roll and the elbow bends slightly as the arm sweeps downwards and outwards.

upwards sweep
As the hand sweeps inline with the shoulder, the palm changes pitch to sweep upwards and inwards. The elbow should then bend to 9o degrees and point to the pool floor.

second downward sweep
The arm action then sweeps inwards towards the thigh and the palm faces downwards. The bent arm action is completed with the arm fully extended and the hand pushing downwards to counter balance the shoulder roll.

recovery
The thumb or the back of the hand should exit the water first. The shoulders roll again with the shoulder of the recovering arm rolling upwards. The arm rotates through 180 degrees over the shoulder. The palm is turned outwards during recovery to ensure that the hand enters the water little finger first.

Common arm pull mistakes

Two common faults cause the arms technique for backstroke to become weak and the overall stroke inefficient.

Firstly the upper arm must brush past the ear and the edge of the hand must enter the water in line with the shoulder. If the hand enters the water wide of the shoulder line then the arm pull with be incomplete and lack power.

Secondly it is very common to perform one arm pull at a time. In other words one arm completes a full arm pull cycle before the second arm begins its arm cycle. The arm pulls for backstroke should be continuous where one arm begins to pull as the other arm begins to recover.

Practicing the arm technique whilst holding a float on the chest is a good way of ensuring the hand is entering inline with the shoulder and that the arm pull is complete. Once this has been mastered then the swimmer can practice the full stroke ensuring the arms are performing continuous cycles.

Breathing during backstroke should be relaxed and easy, due to the supine body position and face being out of the water throughout the stroke. Most swimmers are neither aware of the way in which they breathe, nor the pattern of breathing or point at which a breath is taken.

Breathing should be in time with the recovery of each arm, breathing in with one arm recovery and out with the other. This encourages a breath to be taken at regular intervals.

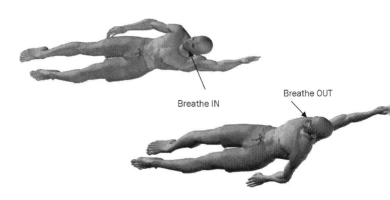

Breathe IN

Breathe OUT

A regular breathing pattern should be encouraged to prevent breath holding, particularly in beginners.

Common breathing mistakes

Breath holding is a common mistake made when swimming this stroke and the result is a very tired and breathless swimmer. Do you ever feel like you become breathless very quickly when swimming this stroke? It goes without saying that swimming contains a very large element of fitness and stamina but this is only one factor.

Breathing technique is essential and it is very common for swimmers, especially beginners to hold their breath without knowing they are doing so.

Performing the stroke slowly at first or with floats to provide support, swimmers must breathe out and then in again in time with each arm pull. Try to establish a rhythm of breathing through each stroke cycle and this will help to prevent breath holding and unnecessary tiredness and exhaustion.

An established breathing rhythm will help to maintain the timing and coordination of the arms and legs as they pull and kick. It will also assist the swimmer to relax and therefore swim with a calm, controlled and smooth backstroke.

Timing

The timing and coordination of the arms and legs develops with practice.

Ideally there should be 6 leg kicks to one arm cycle. The opposite leg kicks downwards at the beginning of each arm pull. This helps to balance the body. This may vary according to the swimmer's level of coordination.

One arm exits the water as the other begins to pull and the
leg kick remains continuous

Arm action should be continuous. i.e. when one arm enters and begins to pull, the other should begin its recovery phase.

Common timing mistakes

A common mistake is performing one arm cycle at a time, resulting in an uneven and unbalanced stroke overall.

Timing and coordination problems occur with backstroke when the legs are allowed to sink below the water surface and the arms lose their continuity and pull one arm at a time.

Counting in your head can sometimes help to maintain stroke rhythm and timing. If you are able to perform a 6 beat cycle then you should count to 3 during each arm pull, therefore kicking 3 legs kicks per arm pull.

If a one beat cycle comes more naturally then there should be one leg kick for each arm pull. Performing the stroke slowly at first will help to establish the rhythm and timing and only when you are proficient swimming at a slow steady pace should you try to increase speed.

With increases in speed comes the greater potential for the timing and coordination to become disrupted and the overall swimming stroke to lose it efficiency.

Backstroke

exercises

BACKSTROKE: Body Position

Floating supine supported by floats

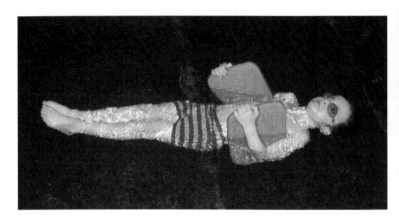

Aim: to gain confidence in a supine position on the water surface.

This exercise is ideal for the nervous swimmer. The teacher or assistant initially can provide support, if he/she is also in the water. 2 floats can then provide support, one placed under each arm, or by a woggle placed under both arms as in the photograph above.

Body position remains level

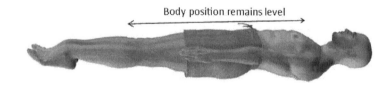

Key Actions

Relax
Make your body flat on top of the water
Keep your head back
Push your tummy up to the surface
Look up to the ceiling
Keep your head still
Keep yourself in a long straight line

Technical Focus

Overall body should be horizontal and streamlined
Head remains still
Eyes looking upwards and towards the feet
Hips must be close to the surface
Legs must be together

Common Faults

Head raises out of the water
Tummy and hips sink
Failing to maintain a flat position

BACKSTROKE: Body Position

Static supine position, holding a single float

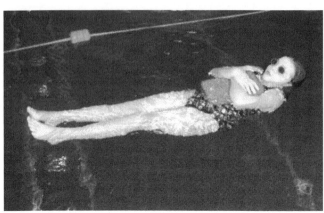

Aim: to develop confidence in a supine position.

Holding a single float across the chest gives security to the nervous swimmer, but is not as stable as a woggle or a float under each arm and so is a subtle and gradual progression. If necessary, this exercise can be performed without a float, as shown in the diagram below, as an additional progression.

Body position remains horizontal and relaxed

Key Actions
Relax
Keep your head back
Push your tummy up to the surface
Look up to the ceiling
Keep your head still

Technical Focus
Overall body should be horizontal
Head remains still
Eyes looking upwards
Hips must be close to the surface
Legs must be together

Common Faults
Head raises out of the water
Eyes look up but head tips forward
Tummy and hips sink
Head moves about
Failing to maintain a straight line

BACKSTROKE: Body Position

Push and glide holding a float

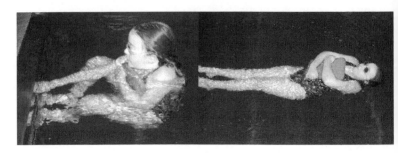

Aim: to gain confidence and move through the water in a supine position.

Holding a float gives added security to the nervous or weak swimmer whilst helping to maintain correct body position.

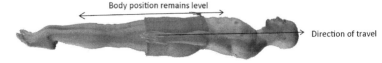

Body position remains level

Direction of travel

Float can be placed on the chest or behind the head as in the photos above.

Key Actions
Relax
Keep your head back and chin up
Push your tummy up to the surface
Look up to the ceiling
Keep your head still
Push off like a rocket

Technical Focus
Overall body should be horizontal and streamlined
Head remains still
Eyes looking upwards
Hips must be close to the surface
Legs must be together

Common Faults
Head raises out of the water
Eyes look up but head tips forward
Tummy and hips sink
Head moves about
Failing to maintain a straight line

BACKSTROKE: Body Position

Push and glide from the poolside without floats

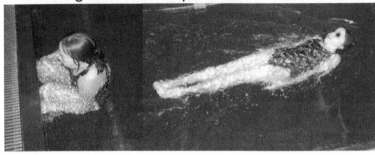

Aim: to encourage correct body position whilst moving.

The swimmer uses the momentum of a push from the poolside. Arms are held by the sides or held straight over the head in more advanced cases.

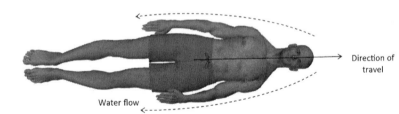

Direction of travel

Water flow

Key Actions
Relax
Make your body as long as you can
Push off like a rocket
Push your tummy up to the surface
Look up to the ceiling
Glide in a long straight line

Technical Focus
Overall body should be horizontal and streamlined
Head remains still
Eyes looking upwards and towards the feet
Hips must be close to the surface
Legs must be together
Arms are held by the sides

Common Faults
Push off is not hard enough
Head raises out of the water
Tummy and hips sink
Failing to maintain a straight line

BACKSTROKE: Legs

Static practice, sitting on the poolside

Aim: to develop an alternating leg kick action.

The swimmer is positioned sitting on the poolside with feet in the water. This is ideal for the nervous beginner to get accustomed to the 'feel' of the water.

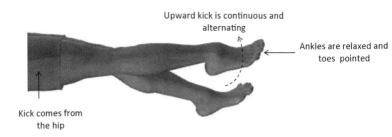

Upward kick is continuous and alternating

Ankles are relaxed and toes pointed

Kick comes from the hip

Key Actions
Point your toes like a ballerina
Kick from your hips
Kick with floppy feet
Keep your legs together
Make your legs as long as possible

Technical Focus
Kick comes from the hips
Toes are pointed
Legs are together
Slight knee bend
Ankles are relaxed

Common Faults
Kick comes from the knee
Legs kick apart
Toes are turned up
Legs are too 'stiff', not relaxed

BACKSTROKE: Legs

Woggle held under the arms

Aim: to practise and develop correct leg kick action.

This exercise is ideal for the nervous beginner as an introduction to swimming on the back. The stability of the woggle encourages kicking and motion backwards with ease.

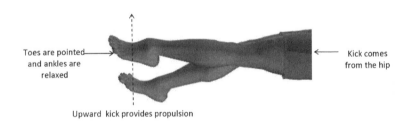

Toes are pointed and ankles are relaxed

Kick comes from the hip

Upward kick provides propulsion

Key Actions
Point your toes like a ballerina
Kick from your hips
Kick with floppy feet
Make a small splash with your toes

Technical Focus
Kick comes from the hips
Kick is alternating and continuous
Kick breaks the water surface
Hips and tummy up near the surface
Toes are pointed and ankles relaxed
Legs are together
Slight knee bend

Common Faults
Kick comes from the knee
Hips sink and legs kick too deep
Toes are turned up
Stiff ankles
Legs are too 'stiff', not relaxed

BACKSTROKE: Legs

Float held under each arm

Aim: to practise and develop leg action whilst maintaining correct body position.

Two floats provide good support and encourage a relaxed body position, without creating excessive resistance through the water.

Body alignment and direction of travel

Continuous alternating upward kick provides propulsion through the water

Key Actions

Relax and kick hard
Point your toes like a ballerina
Kick from your hips
Kick with floppy feet
Make a small splash with your toes
Keep your legs together

Technical Focus

Kick breaks the water surface
Hips and tummy are up near the surface
Toes are pointed and ankles relaxed
Legs are together
Slight knee bend
Ankles are relaxed

Common Faults

Toes are turned up, causing a lack of motion
Head comes up, causing legs to sink
Hips sink and legs kick too deep
Legs kick apart

BACKSTROKE: Legs

Float held on the chest

Aim: to allow the correct body position to be maintained whilst the legs kick.

This is a progression from having a float held under each arm. The swimmer is less stable but still has the security of one float held on the chest.

Ankles are relaxed and toes pointed to provide power to the upward kick

Body position remains level

Kick comes from the hip

Key Actions

Point your toes like a ballerina
Kick from your hips
Kick with floppy feet
Make a small splash with your toes
Keep your legs together

Technical Focus

Kick comes from the hips
Kick is alternating and continuous
Kick breaks the water surface
Hips and tummy up near the surface
Legs are together
Ankles are relaxed and toes pointed

Common Faults

Kick comes from the knee o Legs are too deep
Toes are turned up
Stiff ankles
Legs are too 'stiff', not relaxed

BACKSTROKE: Legs

Float held behind the head

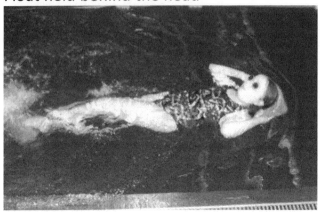

Aim: to encourage correct body position as the legs kick.

The float behind the head helps to keep the chest and hips high. A variation of the exercise with the float held on the chest, this exercise helps to develop leg strength and stamina.

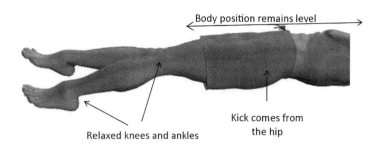

Body position remains level

Kick comes from the hip

Relaxed knees and ankles

Key Actions
Kick from your hips
Kick with floppy feet
Make a small splash with your toes
Keep your legs together

Technical Focus
Kick comes from the hips
Kick breaks the water surface
Hips and tummy up near the surface
Toes are pointed and ankles relaxed
Legs are together

Common Faults
Kick comes from the knee
Legs are too deep
Toes are turned up
Stiff ankles
Legs too 'stiff', not relaxed

BACKSTROKE: Legs

Float held over the knees

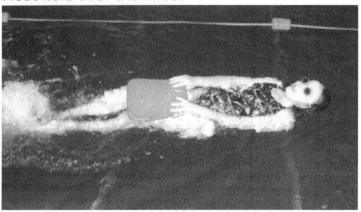

Aim: to prevent excessive knee bend by holding a float over the knees.

This kicking practice should be performed with the float held on the water surface without the knees hitting it as they kick.

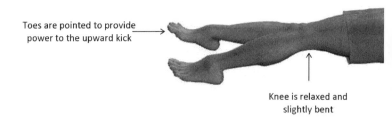

Toes are pointed to provide power to the upward kick

Knee is relaxed and slightly bent

Key Actions
Kick with straight legs
Point your toes like a ballerina
Stop your knees hitting the float
Kick with floppy feet

Technical Focus
Kick comes from the hips
Legs kick without touching the float
Kick breaks the water surface
Hips and tummy up near the surface
Toes are pointed and ankles relaxed

Common Faults
Kick comes from the knee
Knees bend and hit the float
Leg kick is too deep
Float is held up above the water surface

BACKSTROKE: Legs

Float held overhead with arms straight

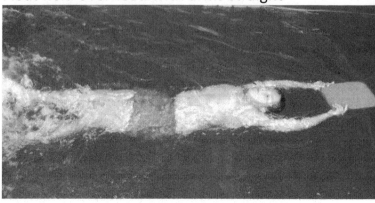

Aim: to enhance a correct body position whilst kicking.

This exercise is a progression from previous leg kick exercises and helps to develop a stronger leg kick.

Legs kick and correct body position is maintained throughout.
Note: advanced alternative is shown without holding a float.

Key Actions
Push your hips and chest up to the surface
Point your toes like a ballerina
Make your whole body long and straight
Kick from your hips
Stretch out and kick hard

Technical Focus
Kick comes from the hips
Arms remain either side of the head
Kick breaks the water surface
Hips and tummy up near the surface

Common Faults
Head is raised causing hips and legs to sink
Hips sink and legs kick too deep
Toes are turned up
Head is too far back and the upper body sinks

BACKSTROKE: Legs

Kicking with arms by the sides, hands sculling

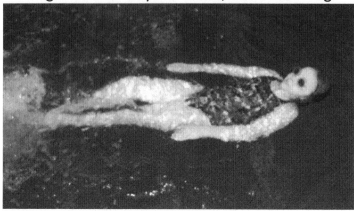

Aim: to practise kicking and maintaining correct body position.

The sculling hand action provides balance and enhances confidence.

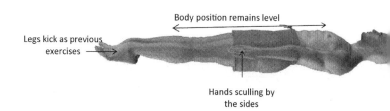

Body position remains level

Legs kick as previous exercises

Hands sculling by the sides

Key Actions
Relax
Push your hips and chest up to the surface
Point your toes like a ballerina
Kick with floppy feet
Look up to the sky

Technical Focus
Kick comes from the hips
Kick is alternating and continuous
Kick breaks the water surface
Hips and tummy up near the surface
Ankles are relaxed and toes are pointed

Common Faults
Kick comes from the knee
Hips sink and legs kick too deep
Head is too far back
Body is not relaxed

BACKSTROKE: Arms

Static practice standing on the poolside

 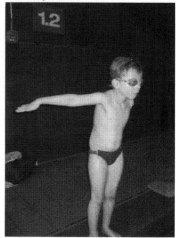

Aim: to practise the arm action in its most basic form.

Standing on the poolside allows the swimmer to develop basic technique in a static position.

Arm rises upwards, little finger leading and arm brushing the ear

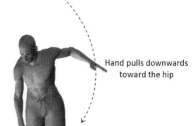

Hand pulls downwards toward the hip

Key Actions
Arms brush past your ear
Fingers closed together
Arms are continuous
Stretch your arm all the way up to your ear
Pull down to your side

Technical Focus
Arm action is continuous
Arms stretch all the way up and brush past the ear
Arms pull down to the side, towards the hip

Common Faults
Arms are not rising to touch the ear
Arms are not pulling down to the side
Pausing in-between arm pulls
Arms are bending over the head

BACKSTROKE: Arms

Single arm pull with a float held on the chest

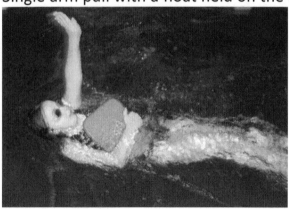

Aim: to develop correct arm action whilst kicking.

The float held on the chest provides support for the beginner and the single arm action allows easy learning without compromising the swimmer's coordination.

Arm exits the water and brushes past the ear, entering the water little finger first

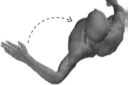

Arm is bent as it pulls through a straightens as it pulls to the thi

Key Actions
Arm brushes past your ear
Pull down to your thigh
Fingers closed together
Little finger enters the water first

Technical Focus
Arm action is continuous
Arms stretch all the way up and brush past the ear
Arms pull down to the thigh
Fingers are together
Little finger enters water first

Common Faults
Arms are pulling out too wide, not brushing the ear
Arms are not pulling down to the side
Arms pull too deep under the water
Fingers are apart
Thumb enters the water first

BACKSTROKE: Arms

Single arm pull using the lane rope

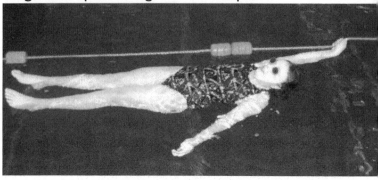

Aim: to develop a bent arm pull using the lane rope to move though the water.

The hand remains fixed on the lane rope as the body is pulled along in the line of the rope. This simulates the bent arm pull action.

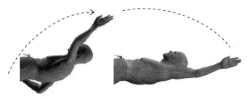

Arm exits the water and brushes past the ear, entering the water little finger first, taking hold of the lane rope

Swimmer pulls from above the head and then pushes past the hip to simulate the bent arm pull action

Key Actions

Use the rope to pull you along
Arms brush past your ear
Stretch over and hold the rope behind
Pull fast down the rope
Thumb comes out first
Little finger enters the water first

Technical Focus

Arm action is continuous
Arms stretch all the way up and brush past the ear
Arms pull down to the thigh
Arm action is continuous
Thumb comes out first

Common Faults

Arms are not pulling down to the side
Elbow is not bending enough
Arms are bending over the head
Thumb enters the water first

BACKSTROKE: Arms

Single arm pull with the opposite arm held by the side

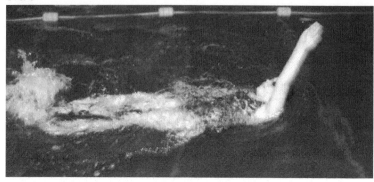

Aim: to practise correct arm action without the aid of floats.

This single arm exercise allows focus on one arm whilst the arm held by the side encourages correct body position.

Arm rises upwards, little finger leading and arm brushing the ear

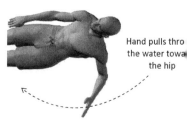

Hand pulls thro the water towa the hip

Key Actions
Arms brush past your ear
Arms are continuous
Pull down to your side
Pull fast through the water
Little finger enters the water first

Technical Focus
Arm action is continuous
Arms stretch all the way up and brush past the ear
Arms pull down to the thigh
Shoulders rock with each arm pull
Little finger enters the water first

Common Faults
Arms are pulling out too wide, not brushing the ear
Arms are not pulling down to the side
Arms pull too deep under the water
Arms are bending over the head

BACKSTROKE: Arms

Arms only with pull-buoy held between legs

Aim: to develop a continual arm action using both arms.

The pull-buoy provides support and helps to isolate the arms by preventing the leg kick action. Note: it is normal for the legs to 'sway' from side to side during this exercise.

Continual arm action causes an even rocking of the shoulders

Key Actions
Arms brush past your ear
Fingers closed together
Continuous arm action
Pull hard through the water and down to your side
Allow your legs to 'sway' side to side

Technical Focus
Arm action is continuous and steady
Arms stretch all the way over and brush past the ear
Arms pull down to the thigh
Shoulders rock evenly side to side

Common Faults
Pause between arm pulls
Arms are pulling out too wide, not brushing the ear
Arms are not pulling down to the side
Arms pull too deep under the water

BACKSTROKE: Breathing

Full stroke with breathing

Aim: to focus on breathing in time with the stroke actions.

The swimmer should breathe in and out in regular rhythm with the arm action. This exercise can be incorporated into any of the previous arm action exercises, depending on the ability of the swimmer.

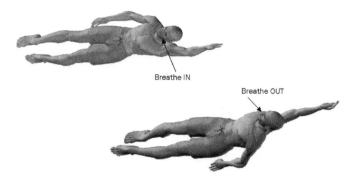

Breathe IN

Breathe OUT

Key Actions
Breathe in time with your arms
Breathe in with one arm pull and out with the other

Technical Focus
Breathing should be regular and rhythmical

Common Faults
Holding the breath
Breathing too rapidly

BACKSTROKE: Timing

Push and glide adding arms and legs

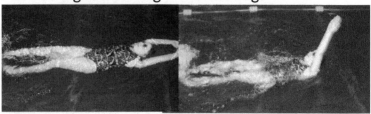

Aim: to practise and develop coordination and stroke timing.

The swimmer performs a push and glide to establish correct body position, then adds arm and leg actions.

One arm exits the water as the other begins to pull and the
leg kick remains continuous

Key Points
Count in your head to 3 with each arm pull
Kick 3 times with each arm pull
Keep the arm pull continuous
Keep the leg kick continuous

Technical Focus
3 leg kicks per arm pull
Leg kick should be continuous
Arm action should be regular

Common Faults
One leg kick per arm pull ('one beat cycle')
Continuous leg kick but not enough arm pulls
Arm pull is too irregular
Stroke cycle is not regular and continuous

BACKSTROKE

Full stroke

Aim: to demonstrate full stroke backstroke showing continuous and alternating arm and leg actions, with correct timing, resulting in a smooth and efficient stroke.

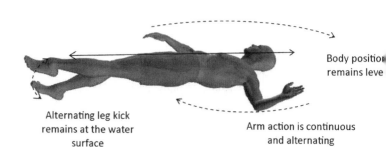

Body position remains level

Alternating leg kick remains at the water surface

Arm action is continuous and alternating

Key Actions

Kick from your hips
Relax
Keep your hips and tummy at the surface
Make a small splash with your toes
Continuous arm action
Arms brush past your ear and pull to your side

Technical Focus

Body position should be horizontal and flat
Leg kick should be continuous and alternating
Arm action is continuous
Leg kick breaks the water surface
3 legs kicks per arm pull

Common Faults

Hips and abdomen sink
Legs kick too deep or weak
Arms pull one at a time
Arms pull too wide or too deep

Backstroke

common questions

Problems and difficulties come from the fact that swimming on your back means you cannot see where you are going! Sounds obvious but when we swim in a prone position (on our front facing forwards) we can see around us and therefore are totally aware of our surroundings. Swimming along whilst facing the sky and we lose most of our surrounding awareness.

Without knowing we then lift our head slightly and this instantly causes the hips to drop and then the legs and the rest of the body follow on, the result: that sinking feeling.

How do I prevent myself from sinking?
When swimming backstroke ensure your head is back enough that your ears are submerged. Then stretch out so that your hips, legs and feet come to the surface. Your leg kick should break the water surface enough to produce a small splash.

Do not fall into the trap of trying at look for your feet or at your flat body position. Moving your head only the slightest inch to check will instantly result in that sinking feeling again. If you can feel your toes breaking the water surface then the chances are your body position is somewhere near correct.

How do I relax on my back and why do I not float when swimming backstroke?

Floating is a characteristic of the human body. Some of us float well and some of us simply do not. It is all down to relative density. Basically fat floats and muscle sinks, which is why lean or muscular people tend to sink.

Focus on your backstroke swimming technique and remaining in the correct position at the water surface will take care of itself.

Become more relaxed in a supine position (on your back) in the water by floating in a star position, with arms and legs wide. This wide body position help you to remain afloat and therefore relax. Even if you are a poor floater, the ability to relax will help all aspect of your backstroke swimming.

"Now that you have finished my book, would you please consider writing a review? Reviews are the best way readers discover great new books. I would truly appreciate it."

Mark Young

For more information about learning to swim and improving your swimming strokes and swimming technique visit:

swim-teach.com

"The number one resource for learning to swim and improving swimming technique."

www.swim-teach.com

Printed in Great Britain
by Amazon